I get it. There is nothing you love more than your children. They bring happiness, joy and purpose to your life.

However, there are times when parenting just gets over-whelming, am I right? Maybe your kids even turn into little monsters and wreak absolute havoc on your day.

For those moments, I present to you the **Swear Word Coloring Book for Parents**.

This adult coloring book is filled with phrases that you many not say directly to your kids, but admit it….you have thought some of them once, twice, or 300 times.

So, just relax and let your inner-parent out with the **Swear Word Coloring Book for Parents**.

NOTE: Designs are printed single-sided for your coloring convenience.

Check out **SwearWordColoringBook.com** for free adult coloring pages and info on all of my books.

Don't forget to sign up to the email list and receive free goodies from time to time!

Happy fucking coloring.

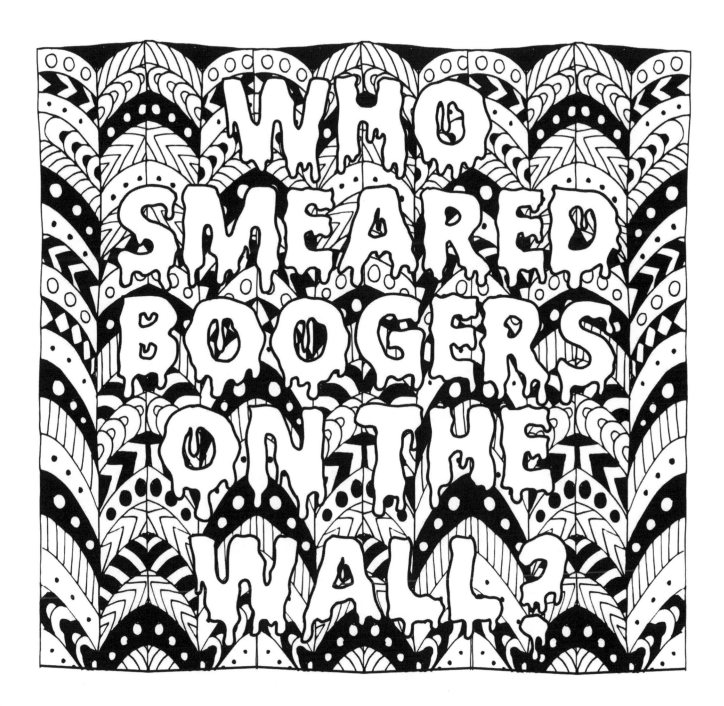

Fuck! Nothing left to color.

But...

...if you want more to color, buy one of these titles from John T!

Made in the USA
Middletown, DE
17 January 2023